Poetry Writing
by Peggy Hapke Lewis

TABLE OF CONTENTS

Teacher Suggestions

The pages in this book may be used as a unit on poetry. However, the pages are especially effective when the study and writing of poetry is braided throughout the school year and across all areas of the curriculum. Ideas for using poetry in many subject areas are included on pages 17 and 18.

Reading and Sharing Poetry

You may choose to read a poem each day to your students. It will help your students to grow accustomed to the rhythms, sounds and varied language patterns of poetry. It is important to choose poems which appeal to children and which vary in length, style and subject matter. Encouraging students to bring in and/or read a poem also adds to the students' anticipation and enjoyment of the daily poem and to the pleasure they take in hearing and writing poetry. Books containing possible poetry selections are suggested on most resource pages in this book.

It is important to expose children to all kinds of poetry, including that written by teachers, published poets and others. Many teachers have had great results from sharing other students' poetry. Examples of student poetry are scattered throughout this book.

If at all possible, have a poet come to your classroom to work with your students. A poet-in-residence would be best. Such artists are available through local arts councils, or check with the National Endowment for the Arts. If funding is a problem, a local poet might be willing to come into the classroom for a nominal fee. It is a good idea to preview the poetry a poet plans to present to be sure it is appropriate for your students.

Even without a visit from a poet, you can do a lot to promote a love of poetry. When reading poetry aloud to children, be sure you have read it aloud to yourself a few times first. Read with feeling and use a natural voice. Hesitate slightly at the ends of lines, a bit longer at a comma, and even longer at a period.

Discussing Poetry

When discussing poems allow children to tell you what the poem meant to them. Ask if students remember any specific lines. Tell them that when they write poems they will recognize lines that are especially good because those will be the lines listeners remember after hearing the poem.

All students may not like the same poem, just as all people may not like the same book. If a student does not like a particular poem, you might ask for details on why he or she does not. Students might also suggest ways a poem could be improved.

Avoid asking too many questions about a poem. A great way to discuss a poem is to have everyone, including the teacher, write for five or ten minutes on what the poem meant to them. This writing can be kept in special poetry journals students use throughout the year. The journals could also hold the poetry students create and collect.

Students may choose to share their written poetry responses with one another. You will be amazed at the different ways children approach a poem and at the varied responses they will draw from it. Each person brings his or her own experiences and knowledge to a poem and takes away a unique reaction.

Memorizing Poetry

Making a child memorize poem after poem can kill the love of poetry. Memorizing poetry should only be done for a specific purpose that can be explained to students. One of the main advantages of memorizing a poem is that the poem becomes a permanent part of a bank of language patterns a child can draw upon forever.

Always be sure the class understands the meaning of a poem before asking them to memorize it. It is a rare child who will speak up and say he or she does not understand, so some gentle questioning may be in order.

There are several ways to encourage memorization without causing undo stress in children with poor memories. One way is to break a long poem into parts and have groups of children memorize portions of it and then perform it together. After several practices, most of the students will have "accidentally" memorized the entire poem. It also helps to have students choose the poem that they will memorize (from a teacher-selected list).

If a whole class is learning a poem, an overhead projector is useful. Many children learn more quickly when they see and hear the poem simultaneously. Have the class recite the poem a few times. Then experiment with covering up a word here or a line there to see how many can remember the missing parts.

Writing Poetry

When students are writing poetry, encourage them to use as broad a vocabulary as possible. Being lenient on spelling requirements will encourage this. Let children know they do not have to spell perfectly in their first drafts. They may initially spell the word the way they think it should be spelled and then later check spellings with a dictionary.

The more students immerse themselves in poetry through active participation in acting out, reciting, writing, memorizing, hearing and reading poems, the better the chance is that students will develop a love and enjoyment of poetry that will last a lifetime. It is our hope that the activities and materials in this book will make it easier for the teacher to teach and enjoy poetry with his or her students.

Warming Up to Poetry

Skills:

a. reading and discussing poetry
b. writing poetry
c. identifying and avoiding clichés

Vocabulary:

sublime, gamboling, prose, cliché, stanzas

Preparation:

Ask which poems are children's favorites. Discuss what topics poems can be about, then tell students that a poem can even be about "nothing." Read aloud the following poem by fourth-grader Jeremy Schoenfeld.

How to Do Nothing
Nothing is something quite easy to do.
Just sit around and watch TV.
Nothing is something parents don't like
*   you to do.*
But I do it anyway, just the same as you.

Ask students what subjects they might enjoy writing about in a poem.

Extension Activities:

Caging Clichés

Tell students to avoid using clichés in their poetry. Have them make a collection of the clichés they find in books, on TV, in everyday speech, etc. Include old, tired similes and metaphors too, such as *busy as a bee*.

Display the clichés. Have students "use them up" by writing poetry that contains the tired sayings. Then tell students they need to use fresh sayings for the rest of the year.

Two-Word Poetry

This is a great warm-up for all students, including reluctant poets. Write the following poem on the board and have a student read it aloud.

Birds fly
above us.
White bellies
like hands
in water.

Explain that the poem is a simple description of how flying birds look to a poet. Work with your class to write another poem with two words per line. Then ask students to write two or three more of these poems and share them.

It's Not As It Seems

Have students write a poem that initially seems to be about one topic and then turns out to be about another. Here is an example:

Crowds jostling, laughing, bumping
through the stores, filling their bags
with presents and candy
while I lie here in my heated bed
and shiver.

Weather or Not

Review weather poems, such as "Rain, rain, go away" or "It's raining, it's pouring." Have students help you change the poems' weather in some way (e.g., "It's sleeting, it's snowing...").

Bulletin Board:

Make a display of tired sayings behind bars to reinforce the idea that students should not use them.

Books to Look for:

Larrick, Nancy. *Piping Down the Valleys Wild.* Dell, 1968. Interesting poems to read aloud.
Worth, Valerie. *Small Poems.* Farrar Straus, 1972. Short, witty poems.

Activity Sheet Answers (p. 5):

4. *Sublime* means grand or splendid.
5. *Gamboling* means skipping around at play.
Other answers will vary.

Warming Up to Poetry

Prose is the everyday language people use when they speak or write. One difference between prose and poetry is that poetry is divided into lines. Also, close attention is paid to the sounds of words in poetry. Another difference is that poetry has to say a great deal in a limited amount of words and space. Each line of a poem is important to the sound and meaning of the poem.

Some people think all poetry rhymes and is about topics like love and flowers. Actually, poems can take many different forms and can be about any topic.

Read the poem below and answer the questions that follow it.

How Do You Come to a Poem?

I come to poetry as a cat
rummaging through piles.
Avoiding bitter peels
I tug at specks of meat,
sublime treats I feel
were buried there for me.
A poem is perfect
if I come away with one
good taste of tuna.
But I never get my fill.

Sometimes I come as a monkey
to climb among the stanzas
and swing by skinny limbs on lines
that spring and shine
but never drop.
It's hard to stop
when hand over paw
I'm moving through ideas
that expand, grow curly vines
that whirl and twirl.
More fun than food this
gamboling on a poem.

1. Which lines of the poem do you like best? Why? _____
   _____

2. How does the writer feel about a poem? _____
   _____

3. Give three examples of words in the poem that rhyme or sound similar in some way.
   _____

4. What does *sublime* mean? _____ What does the word tell you
   about the cat's opinion of meat? _____

5. What does the word *gamboling* mean? _____
   Why is it a good word choice for the poem? _____
   _____

6. What kinds of poetry do you like to read?_____

7. Think of your favorite person, place, or thing. Jot down ideas about what it is you
   like about your choice. Then use your notes to create a short poem.

The Richness of Poetry

Skills:
a. understanding the crafting of poems
b. using the five senses to enrich poetry

Vocabulary:

marshmallow (review spelling), *nickers*

Preparation:

Blindfold students and give each one a large marshmallow. Ask students to suggest words and phrases which describe the marshmallows. They should describe the feel, sound (when squeezed lightly), smell, and finally taste. Write their descriptions on the chalkboard.

Extension Activities:

Marshmallow Writing
Have students use the words collected in the activity above to write marshmallow poetry.

> *Tiptoe on a powdery sweet*
> *marshmallow in bare feet.*
> *Feel the skin-soft surface*
> *of the spongy cake of white.*

Toothpick Poems
Give each student a generous supply of toothpicks and miniature marshmallows. Have them build a structure and write a poem about it. Builders can display their creations and read their poems one at a time.

Poetry Walk Around the Block
Have students carry poetry notebooks and write (in detail) what they see, hear, smell, and feel as they walk outside the school building.

Square-Foot Poems
Give each child a 48" piece of string. Have them stretch it into a square on the ground. Ask students to list everything they see inside the square and then write poetry about the sights.

> *The ant glides along a leaf like three*
> *steel balls in a green groove.*
> *I wonder if he likes the ride when the*
> *breeze makes his world move.*

Mixing the Senses
Have students write a poem which starts with a line that mixes the senses, such as, "Poison ivy screamed at me from my arms and legs." (A feeling is heard in this line.)

Searching for Sense
Bring in books of poetry. Ask students to use them to find examples of how poets use the five senses in different ways. Discuss how the poems would be different if the senses were not used.

Bulletin Board:

Put an interesting photograph on the bulletin board. Have students surround it with sensory descriptions, using as many of the five senses as possible. Also, put up poems in which poets create imagery which appeals to the senses.

Why I Love Horses
> *Sharp hooves pounding the pasture,*
> *wavy mane and tail sailing out behind.*
> *Low nickers as I walk into the stable*
> *and a velvet nose nuzzling my cheek.*
> *The smell of sweet, warm fur*
> *as I reach to unlatch his cheek strap.*

Books to Look for:

Ferris, Helen. *Favorite Poems Old and New.* Doubleday, 1957. Many and varied poems selected by Helen Ferris.

Janeczko, Paul. *The Delicious Day: Sixty-Five Poems.* Orchard Books, 1987. Collection compiled by Paul Janeczko.

Activity Sheet Answers (p. 7):

1. hearing, touch, sight
Other answers will vary.

The Richness of Poetry

A poem is like gold. When a poet thinks of an idea for a poem it is like seeing a vein of gold in a mine. The poet puts words on paper, just as a miner chips out chunk after chunk of gold ore. Like valuable gold is separated from the ore, a poet keeps the good parts of a poem and gets rid of the weaker parts, removing imperfections and polishing it. Finally, like a golden ring, the final product, a poem, may appeal to some people and not to others, but it has reached its final form.

As infants, the only way we could take in information was through the senses. Even as adults it is often easier to understand language when it relates to the senses. Here is a poem written by a student named Laurie Carkeet when she was in the fifth grade. Notice how she uses the five senses to enhance her poem.

You Were on My Mind

*I thought I heard your name
but it was only the soft tread
of the butterfly.
I thought I felt your hair
but it was only the feather
from a solitary bird passing by.
I thought I saw your image
but it was only a flicker
of a rainbow left from spring.
I thought I felt your touch
but it was only the wind floating by.
I saw you where you never were.
You were on my mind.*

1. Which senses does the author use in her poem? _____
_____

2. Rewrite the poem using your own examples of how your senses could fool you into thinking someone was near.

_____
_____
_____
_____
_____
_____

3. Imagine being blindfolded in the dungeon of a castle. Write a poem which will make readers feel they are actually there.

_____
_____
_____
_____
_____
_____
_____

The Rhythm of Poetry

Skills:

a. understanding iambic, trochaic, anapestic and dactylic meter
b. understanding the poetic foot

Vocabulary:

meter, free verse, poetic foot

Preparation:

The rhythm in poetry is referred to as *meter*. Have students march, clap or tap a pencil to the rhythm of a favorite poem with a solid beat. Discuss the relationship between poetry and music. (Students should note that music has a certain number of beats per measure, and metrical poetry contains a certain number of accented and unaccented syllables per line.)

Extension Activities:

Very Poetic Feet!

To help reinforce the concept of a poetic foot, cut large foot shapes out of construction paper. Next, using a metrical poem students are familiar with, write the poem putting each poetic foot, with its accented and unaccented syllables, on a separate foot shape.

Allusion

Some poets use favorite poems by other authors to spark their own poetry. This is called allusion. The poet alludes, or refers, to the other poet's poem, and often mentions the poem or poet in the title.

To William with Love
Where the poet lurks, I lie.
In a book I live and die.
There I hide while days pass by.
In a world of words dwell I.

This poem alludes to William Shakespeare's famous poem "Fairy Life" which begins,

"Where the bee sucks, there suck I." It employs the same metrical pattern.

Tell students that when they write a poem like this, it is important to mention the writer and the name of the poem to which they allude.

Omitting Meter

Choose a poem with very definite meter. Ask students to rewrite it changing words, lines and meter without changing the poem's meaning. Ask how the changes affect the poem. Is it better or worse?

Bulletin Board:

• Display the feet from the "Very Poetic Feet" activity.
• Display large copies of poems with different metrical patterns. Mark the accented and unaccented syllables with neon markers.

Books to Look for:

Drury, John. *Creating Poetry*. Writer's Digest Books, 1991. Valuable information on the craft of poetry.

Activity Sheet Answers (pp. 9 & 10):

Page 9
Number of poetic feet in "I knew a man..." is 4.
Mary had a little lamb.
Its fleece was white as snow.
And everywhere that Mary went
The lamb was sure to go.

Page 10   Nursery rhymes will vary.
Down in the valley where the green grass grows,
there sat Edna, sweet as a rose.
She sang, she sang, she sang so sweet.
Along came Ted and kissed her on the cheek.
How many kisses did he give her? One, Two, ..."

The Rhythm of Poetry

The way a poem moves is called its rhythm. All poetry has a rhythm. It may be **metrical**, (with counted beats per line), **free verse** (with no fixed pattern of meter or rhyme), or even **prose** (ordinary written language).

Our everyday speech has rhythm, or meter. The most common meter in poetry, **iambic meter**, is often used in everyday speech. Iambic meter consists of an unstressed syllable followed by a stressed syllable (sounding like *ta-dum*).

Example: I **don't** know **why** you **nev**er **make** your **bed**.

Shakespeare used this natural rhythm in much of his poetry. The example above is a pentameter, the most common length of iambic meter . A pentameter contains five iambic feet in a line (five sets of an unstressed and a stressed syllable).

Each time your voice rises and falls with a group of two or three syllables with the accent on one of the syllables that is called a **poetic foot**. Think of it as a way of walking through the poem. The example above contains five poetic feet. How many poetic feet are there in each line of the following poem? _____

I **knew** a **man** who **had** a **plan**
to **build** a ro**bot strong** and **grand**
But **when** the ro**bot was** all **done**
He **found** it **did** the **work** of **none**.

The rhythm of a poem often creates a response in readers.
Jack and Jill went up the hill to fetch a pail of water.
Jack fell down and broke his crown, and Jill came tumbling after.

Even tiny children enjoy the regular beat, or rhythm, of nursery rhymes. To figure out the meter of this popular nursery rhyme, decide which syllables are stressed, or on which syllables your voice sounds louder or higher. Those are the accented syllables. To mark meter, place a long mark —— over accented (stressed) syllables and a short mark ⌣ over unaccented (unstressed) syllables:

— ⌣ — ⌣ — ⌣ —
Jack fell down and broke his crown.

Notice that each metrical foot is made up of a stressed syllable followed by an unstressed syllable. This is **trochaic meter**, one of the most commonly used meters.

Mark the stressed and unstressed syllables in this first verse of "Mary Had a Little Lamb."

Mary had a little lamb.

Its fleece was white as snow.

And everywhere that Mary went

The lamb was sure to go.

9

The Rhythm of Poetry (cont.)

Make up your own nursery rhyme that contains trochaic meter, the meter used in "Jack and Jill."

_____

_____

_____

_____

Another common meter is **anapestic meter**. The anapest consists of two unaccented syllables and one accented syllable which results in a kind of galloping sound.

Example: In the **morn**ing the **sun** shines so **warm** on my **face**.

A very familiar poem written in anapestic meter begins, "'Twas the night before Christmas and all through the house...."

Dactylic meter consists of one stressed syllable followed by two unstressed syllables.

Example: **Where** are the **flow**ers that **bloom** in the **spring**?

Mark the meter on this familiar jump-rope rhyme which combines several different meters.

Down in the valley where the green grass grows,

There sat Edna, sweet as a rose.

She sang, she sang, she sang so sweet

Along came Ted and kissed her on the cheek.

How many kisses did he give her?   One, Two..."

Read the following poem.
Listen to the rise and fall of your voice.

Mary Martha Mumblety-peg
Had an ache in her left leg.

She had a pony with the gout
And seven limping pigs about.

She called the doctor for advice
But he just said, "Stay home! Eat rice!"

Practice your sense of rhythm by writing a modern jump-rope rhyme on the back of this paper.

10   POETRY WRITING

The Sound of Poetry

Skills:

Understanding the use of sound devices in poetry

Vocabulary:

alliteration,   assonance,   consonance, onomatopoeia

Preparation:

Ask if students know any tongue twisters. Ask one or two students to recite one, or use one of the old faithfuls such as "Peter Piper picked a peck of pickled peppers." Write a line or two of a tongue twister on the board and talk about the repetition of sounds. Make up a new classroom tongue twister if time permits.

Extension Activities:

Alliteration on a Theme

Write a theme, such as *forests*, at the top of the chalkboard. Have students work individually or in groups to make lists of words with the same initial consonant sounds that are connected in some way with the theme (ex. forests—rocks, rain, rivers, raccoons). Then have students write poems using the words they've collected.

Repetition Mission

Read this poem to students:

*Who sails the unknown seas
in calm or stormy weather?
Patrick Penn the Pirate.
Patrick Penn the Pirate.*

*Who has a leg of wood
and wears a shirt of leather?
Patrick Penn the Pirate.
Patrick Penn the Pirate.*

Ask who can repeat the poem as accurately

as possible, and then discuss how repetition as well as the pattern of the poem makes this poem easier to remember than others. Have students add a stanza or two and recite the poem creatively, with individuals and groups of students taking various parts of the poem. Have the class work in pairs to create original poems using effective repeating lines.

Sound Effect

Play a wide variety of classical music and have students write poetry that shares the mood of the music. Vivaldi's *Four Seasons* is light and cheery. Rachmaninoff is great for drama. Have students read their poems and have others guess the music to which it was written.

Bulletin Board:

Make an acrostic by writing the word *onomatopoeia* vertically on a bulletin board. Have the class think of an onomatopoeia that begins with each letter in the word *onomatopoeia*.

Books to Look for:

Merriam, Eve. *Out Loud*. Athenium, 1973.
Prelutsky, Jack. *The Snopp on the Sidewalk*. William Morrow & Co., 1977, 1978.

Activity Sheet Answers (pp. 12 & 13):

Page 12
Answers will vary. The following are sample answers only.
1. <u>s</u>ouls who <u>s</u>igh
2. r<u>o</u>w a b<u>oa</u>t
3. <u>s</u>addle on a <u>s</u>ea horse ye<u>s</u>terday.

Page 13
in a dentist's office

The Sound of Poetry

Poems are meant to be heard. Poets use several devices to achieve certain sound effects in a poem. **Alliteration** is commonly used. This is the repetition of the beginning consonants, as in "Cathy can catch a cat." This sentence also happens to contain **assonance** which is the repetition of a vowel sound. The short *a* sound is repeated.

Headlines and advertisements often use these devices because they grab readers' attention and make words or phrases easy to remember. A sports headline may read "Owls Oust Oilers!" or an ad may announce "Sensational Salami Sale!" When the repeated consonant sound is not always at the beginning of the word, the device is called **consonance**: The moon shone through Nina's window.

Complete the following lines with appropriate words.
1. Alliteration: Speak softly of _____ who _____.
2. Assonance: Joe can _____ a _____or he can make it float.
3. Consonance: Doris put a _____ on a _____horse _____.

Sometimes poets repeat entire words as well as sounds. Notice the effect fourth-grader Elizabeth Robinson created by repeating words in her poem.

The Unicorn
Through wind and rain I gallop,
Stronger every day.
Eating only wild grass and berries
Tired as I lay.
Nobody can catch me,
Nobody dares,
For I am wild,
Wild as the night,
Wild as the long, lonely night.

Write a poem containing at least one of the poetic devices explained on this page.

_____

_____

_____

_____

_____

_____

_____

_____

Onomatopoeia

Onomatopoeia refers to words which sound like the sound or action they describe. These words imitate the natural sounds associated with the object or action involved, such as *bang, hiss, smack, clink,* or *buzz.*

*Gerald heard a click as the whir began
then a buzz and the bang of a metal pan.
He opened wide and heard a clink,
a gurgle and a splat like a stopped-up sink.*

From the sounds described, where do you think Gerald was? _____

Different sounds are associated with different places. Write a few onomatopoeic words you might hear at

a baseball game	a school	a zoo
_____	_____	_____
_____	_____	_____
_____	_____	_____
_____	_____	_____
_____	_____	_____

What is another place you can think of where you would hear many different sounds? _____ Make a list of those sounds and use them in a poem. Don't name the place you are describing. If you have captured the place with onomatopoeia, your readers should know what place it is.

Onomatopoeia   **Poem**

_____   _____

_____   _____

_____   _____

_____   _____

_____   _____

                   POETRY WRITING

Imagery

Skills:

a. how to use imagery
b. understanding similes
c. understanding metaphors

Vocabulary:

imagery, filigree, simile, metaphor

Preparation:

Ask students to imagine that a huge tree has fallen through the classroom window, without hitting anyone. Ask students how they would describe the occurrence. Have volunteers try to tell the most exciting version of the story. Then ask a volunteer to tell about the event without using any descriptive words. Talk about the effectiveness of imagery in writing or speech.

Extension Activities:

Colorful Images!

A fun way to think of images for poems is to make a list of ideas that relate to a word. This writer, for example uses the word *blue*.

*Blue is for billiard balls, bird eggs and blue
   jeans,
Blue skies and rivers and lakes.
Blue is for butterflies, marbles and my eyes
and even the blue racer snake.*

Mood from Images

Have a student read aloud the poem at the top of the Imagery worksheet (p. 15). Ask what mood the poem evokes (loneliness, sadness, etc.). Ask what images and words contribute to that feeling (Images: silver cobwebs in dim moonlight, wolf howling, shadows. Words: *cobweb, half moon, lone wolf, howled, owl cry, alone, lurked, shadows*).

Choose a mood and have students write words that evoke that mood. Then ask them to write a short poem loaded with words and images which will convey the mood.

Similar Similes

Read sixth-grader Tom Robinson's poem to students and ask them if they can spot the simile (sun sprouted like a flower).

*The morning was gloomy.
Everything was gray and blue
as far as the eye could see.
Suddenly the sun sprouted
from the horizon like a
flower in my garden
brightening my soul.*

Ask how the simile could be turned into a metaphor (the sun was a flower). Put students in pairs to write short poems containing similes.

Bulletin Board:

Put up pictures, drawings or actual objects such as seashells or pinecones. Around these images, have students list things the objects could stand for as metaphors. For example, a seashell could be a home or a barrier around our feelings.

Books to Look for:

Kuskin, Karla. *Near the Window Tree: Poems and Notes.* Harper, 1975.
Larrick, Nancy. ed., *Green is Like a Meadow of Grass: An Anthology of Children's Pleasure in Poetry.* Garrard, 1968.

Activity Sheet Answers (pp. 15 & 16):

Page 15
2. like a prizefighter, as fast as a conductor leading an orchestra, like a blue crab

Page 16
1. Friendship is compared to chocolate.
2. The metaphor lets the reader know Billy loved his friends.
3. Other metaphors for friendship might include water in the desert or the sun in winter.

Name _____

Imagery

The word **imagery** comes from *image* and refers to creating a visual picture. Imagery allows readers to understand what a writer is saying because they can picture a scene in their minds. One way to present an image is to use physical description:

> *Cobwebs of silver filigree*
> *barely lit by the half moon shone*
> *as one lone wolf howled his long, owl cry*
> *and I, alone, lurked among the shadows.*

Similes

Another way to present an image is to compare something to something else. The sentence "The old man danced <u>like</u> a child jumping rope" creates a more exact image than "The old man was light on his feet as he danced." We call a comparison which includes the words *like* or *as* a **simile**. The name comes from the Latin word *similis* meaning similar.

1. Similes are a wonderful way to play with language. Think of a cliché such as *green as grass*. Now think of ten original similes for the adjective you have chosen.

_____   _____

_____   _____

_____   _____

_____   _____

_____   _____

> *The cat entered the room like a prizefighter.*
> *He pumped his balled-up paws up and down*
> *as fast as a conductor leading the orchestra.*
> *Just before he reached the Pekinese in the corner,*
> *who cringed and backed up like a blue crab,*
> *the cat dropped to all fours and smiled.*

2. What similes can you find in the cat poem above? _____

_____

3. Write a poem that contains at least three similes.

_____

_____

_____

Name _____

Metaphors

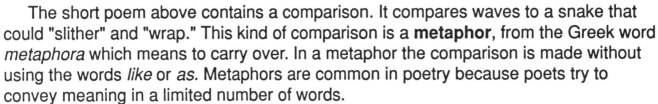

White waves slithered across the beach,
wrapped around the black rocks
then slipped back to the sea.

The short poem above contains a comparison. It compares waves to a snake that could "slither" and "wrap." This kind of comparison is a **metaphor**, from the Greek word *metaphora* which means to carry over. In a metaphor the comparison is made without using the words *like* or *as*. Metaphors are common in poetry because poets try to convey meaning in a limited number of words.

A student named William R. Ray, Jr. used a metaphor in this poem he wrote in sixth grade.

Walking into the room
was walking into chocolate.
The sweet fall air
fluttered the leaves in soft colors.
A choir of birds warmed up
on the balcony of branches.
In the school yard is where

what was important happened.
The sweet taste
of unbreakable friendship.
I could then see into every person,
and what I saw was
beauty...

1. What metaphor did William use in his poem? _____

2. How does the metaphor help the reader know how William felt?_____
_____

3. What other metaphors could William have used in his poem?_____
_____

If a writer wants to change a simile to a metaphor, he or she takes out the words *as* or *like* and compares objects by saying one object **is** another.

Examples:
<u>Similes</u>
that child is sweet as an angel
birds flying like kites
taking the test was like being tortured

<u>Metaphors</u>
that child is an angel
the birds were kites in the sky
the test was a torture chamber

Write a poem that contains at least two metaphors.

_____
_____
_____
_____

Poetry Across the Curriculum

Skills:

using poetry in a variety of disciplines

Preparation:

Ask students what uses poems have. Discuss the fact that poetry can be used for lyrics, greeting cards, signs, gifts, journal entries, books, plays, nursery rhymes, presentations, jokes, letters, and much more. Poems can also help people learn.

Extension Activities:

Out of This World Poetry!

After studying a unit on space or astronomy, have students write poetry about an aspect of space that interests them.

Field Trip Poetry

Upon returning from a field trip have students make notes on what they saw and heard and then write poetry about it. These can be collected in classroom anthologies.

Perplexed Poetry

When students are having difficulty learning a math concept, have them write out the concept and the problems associated with it. Then they can write poetry explaining it to someone else.

Class Starter!

Begin a math class with the poem "Math," written by a girl named Margaret Higgins when she was in the fifth grade.

The multiplication doubles your brain,
The division splits it in half.
The adding helps you re-gain
The brains you'll need in math!

Pick up your pencil and wait
'Til that brain in your head starts to grow.
Then listen to the teacher who'll teach you a
*   lesson,*
And pick up your books to go.

Poetry Painting

Have students paint pictures and write poems to go with them. Cooperation from the art teacher would be helpful.

Environmental Poetry

Have students write poems about saving the rainforest. Display the poems on poster board.

Notes Home

Poems announcing an upcoming event will attract more attention than regular notes home. Have students work together to create poems conveying important information about events.

Current Events Poetry

Have students clip articles about current events and bring them into the classroom. Review the five *w*'s then have students write poetry about the current events.

Bulletin Board:

Display poems written by students and professional poets about various subject areas (math, geography, history, etc.).

Activity Sheet Answers (p. 18):

If students have trouble distinguishing facts from information added for rhyming purposes, discuss the following lines:

Elk spend winter in low mountain valleys
Like cats spend time in dirty, old alleys.

The first line contains a fact about elk. The second is unrelated to the topic of elk, but rhymes with the first line.

Poetry reports may be written in any subject area. Each student should select a different topic. Students need to do fairly extensive research and collect between 30 and 40 facts out of which they must use 25 in the poem.

It is helpful to ask for a bibliography including at least one magazine, one book on the subject, and one reference book when having students write reports.

Poetry Across the Curriculum

There are many reasons for writing poems. Some poems express delight or curiosity about something. Others provide information about a subject. Here is a poem a girl named Margaret Higgins wrote for her science report in fourth grade. She includes at least twenty-five facts about elks.

The Elk

I believe it is winter. I think we will survive.
The thermometer is below zero, but elk will stay alive.

I'm telling you this story because I really care!
Go outside in this elk-cold winter, oh don't you even dare!
The male is seven hundred to one thousand pounds.
He'll lead the whole elk family, in winter, toward low ground.

In spring they'll return up high to a mountain.
Their return is with joy, so they spring up like a fountain!
The largest elk herds live in Yellowstone Park,
Or high in the mountains, in the pitch dark.

When the elk molt their fur, they're smelly and shaggy looking,
So when there's a bad smell, you'll know what's cooking.
In North America, as we've seen,
The elks are rising with the sun's gleam!

When the thermometer's below zero,
For elk it's hard to travel in deep, cold snow.
Elk usually eat grasses that really cure.
They also eat twigs and needles of fir.

Today elks aren't often seen around
But if you're looking, don't look on the ground.
Elk are also called the *wapiti*.
They look the same and are the same species.

They still aren't around as much on a hill
Which means they are hard to find and kill.
In Canada, too, that's one other place, their antlers sheathed in
    thick, velvet fur.
We don't know who they are; they didn't know who we were.

Elk spend winter in low mountain valleys
Like cats spend time in dirty, old alleys.
Some elks do not have enough winter range for feeding.
When they cannot find enough food, you'll often see them
    leaving.

Don't scream when you see an elk, and if you ever think to
Remember if you're afraid of them, they're afraid of you!

1. Underline all the facts about elk.

2. Which parts of the poem do you believe were added to make the rhyme or meter (beats per measure) come out right, rather than to tell about the elk?

   _____
   _____
   _____

3. What do you like about the poem? _____
   _____

4. What would you do differently if you were writing the poem? _____
   _____

Think of a subject you know a great deal about and research it further. Make a list of 30 or 40 facts about the subject. Write a poem that includes at least 25 of the facts.

Limericks and Cinquains

Skills:

a. understanding and writing limericks
b. understanding and writing cinquains

Vocabulary:

limerick, cinquain, anapestic (see The Rhythm of Poetry)

Preparation:

Before beginning a lesson on limericks, read several limericks to students. Write a limerick such as the following one on the board. Have students recite it and then change some of the words, keeping the same meter.

There once was a teacher from Dallas
Who wanted to teach in a palace.
She called up the queen
Who said, "No way! I'm mean."
She hadn't known queens were so callous.

Before beginning a lesson on cinquains, do a free-write with students in which they write on a subject without stopping for five to ten minutes. Then have them underline parts of their writing that appeal to them in some way.

To improve imagery in the cinquains, have students write down images that are beautiful (ugly, frightening, enchanting, etc.). Ask them to describe those images in ways they have never thought of before. (Example: "Her hair was the cinnamon of a red ant's back.")

Extension Activities:

Limerick Teams

Divide students into groups of four or five and challenge them to write limericks about invented characters. It is best to discourage poems about real people to avoid hurt feelings. Have a group sharing session to present finished limericks.

Back to Ireland!

Ask students to find Ireland in an atlas or on a map of the world. Have students copy the names of Irish cities or counties and use them in limericks.

Name Cinquains

Have students choose fictional or real people and write cinquains about them.

Tammy
loves to dance fast
to rock 'n roll music
as she swings her long auburn hair
and sings.

Arthur
wants a swift boat
to sail the ocean blue
on a trip around the whole world
alone.

Scientific Cinquains

Rain Forest

A vast
lush paradise
where medicines are found.
People are destroying them now.
Stop it!

Bulletin Board:

Cut large green shamrocks out of construction paper. In each of the three leaves, write part of a limerick.

Books to Look for:

Lobel, Arnold. *The Book of Pigericks: Pig Limericks.* Harper Collins, 1983.

Cole, Joanna. *A New Treasury of Children's Poetry.* Doubleday, 1984. Over 200 traditional and modern poems and limericks selected by Joanna Cole.

Limericks

The **limerick** was made popular by Edward Lear in his *Book of Nonsense* in 1846. These humorous verses, often containing puns (plays on words), were named after the city of Limerick, Ireland. Limericks are fun to write because they are short and have a catchy rhythm. A limerick contains five lines of mainly anapestic meter (two unaccented syllables and one accented). Lines 1, 2, and 5 rhyme. Lines 3 and 4 are shorter and rhyme with each other. The best way to learn to write a limerick is to read one and follow its pattern.

There once was a lion named Perry
whose coat was all bald and not hairy.
He went to a pig
who made him a wig.
Now Perry's a cat that's quite merry.

Write your own animal limerick using the one above as a pattern. Note the rhyming pattern of AABBA.

_____(A)
_____(A)
_____(B)
_____(B)
_____(A)

When you understand the pattern of the limerick, it's sometimes fun to change it slightly as fourth-grader Matt Kaskowitz did in this funny poem.

<u>The Wart</u>
Hey, you, don't fiddle,
your wart's fairly little,
but you never know if it'll grow.
You better act fast or your finger won't last.
It might grow as big as your toe!

Write a limerick or a limerick-like poem about yourself. If your name is hard to rhyme, avoid including it. For example, the first line for a boy who likes reading might be "There once was a boy who liked books."

_____
_____
_____
_____
_____

Cinquains

The **cinquain** is a popular form of poetry. It consists of twenty-two syllables in a pattern of 2, 4, 6, 8, 2. In a cinquain, as with any poem, the poet tries to use fresh language to capture an image or a feeling.

Blue jay
On the oak deck
Bullies all the finches.
He jumps into the air and they
Are back!

Candles
Light my study
As I pour lonely words
From my heart into letters to
Send you.

The form of the cinquain helps poets express a thought with very few words. This means the poet must choose his or her words carefully. Write two cinquains and then illustrate the one you like best.

_____   _____

_____   _____

_____   _____

_____   _____

The parts-of-speech cinquain is a spin-off of the type of cinquain above. A parts-of-speech cinquain contains five lines, but it does not limit the poet to a certain number of syllables in each line. Instead, this cinquain follows the following form: Line 1 is a noun; line 2 is two words describing the noun; line 3 contains action words telling what the noun does; line 4 includes four words about the noun; and line 5 is one word which refers to the first word. Look at the example below.

Write a parts-of-speech cinquain on the lines below.

Horses
Sleek, fast
Rearing, prancing, neighing
They inhabit my dreams
Forbidden

_____

_____

_____

_____

Imagination and Exaggeration

Skills:

a. stimulating imagination
b. using exaggeration
c. understanding irony
d. understanding satire

Vocabulary:

irony, satire

Preparation:

A great way to stimulate imagination is to use guided imagery. Ask students to close their eyes and imagine they are creeping up into an elderly relative's attic. Tell them they are slowly opening a dusty old trunk, an ancient hatbox, etc. Have children write what they "saw" in each place. Share ideas and discuss the limitless treasure of each person's imagination.

Extension Activities:

Pretzel Poem

Have students write a poem which starts out realistically and then turns into a fantasy poem, such as the following:

> *My grandparents took me to dinner*
> *for pizza because of my grades.*
> *I had pepperoni with extra cheese on it*
> *and that's where the memory fades.*
>
> *The waiter who brought out the pizza*
> *was wearing a white bunny suit.*
> *In fact, he was really a rabbit*
> *and he served my milk in a boot!*

The Poet as Explorer

Tell students that poets are explorers. They begin with an idea, a thought, an image, and then they follow it into their imaginations. There are unlimited connections and directions in our minds. That is why for every idea, every poet could write a different poem. Ask students to write a word that represents something they love, hate, or fear and then draw a circle around it. Then they should write related words as fast as they think of them, circling each word and connecting it to the related word by a line. After ten or fifteen minutes ask students to choose ten interesting words from their diagram and use them in a poem.

Surprise Poetry

Read the following poem to students and ask them what was happening in the poem. Then have them write an original poem containing a surprise.

> *The river was calm, more like a lake,*
> *when Uncle and I went fishing.*
> *I trailed my fingers in the water*
> *And did some powerful wishing.*
>
> *The water broke and something jumped*
> *the size of twenty dolphins.*
> *The creature twisted in the air*
> *and slapped us with its tail fins.*

Impossible Poems

Have kids write impossible poems such as the following:

> *I just got back from somewhere I have never*
> *been.*
> *Luckily, I missed the puddle of mud I just*
> *stepped in.*

Books to Look for:

Silverstein, Shel. *Where the Sidewalk Ends.* Harper & Row, 1974. Hilarious, imaginative poems.

Silverstein, Shel. *A Light in the Attic.* Harper, 1981.

Name _____

Imagination

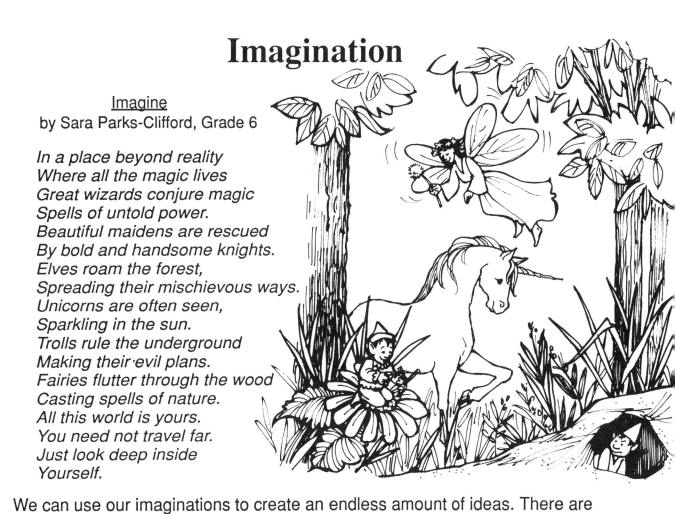

Imagine
by Sara Parks-Clifford, Grade 6

In a place beyond reality
Where all the magic lives
Great wizards conjure magic
Spells of untold power.
Beautiful maidens are rescued
By bold and handsome knights.
Elves roam the forest,
Spreading their mischievous ways.
Unicorns are often seen,
Sparkling in the sun.
Trolls rule the underground
Making their·evil plans.
Fairies flutter through the wood
Casting spells of nature.
All this world is yours.
You need not travel far.
Just look deep inside
Yourself.

We can use our imaginations to create an endless amount of ideas. There are countless ways to weave together imaginative ideas and experiences to create outstanding stories and poems. Sara's poem gives an idea of the kinds of characters and plots that are running around in her imagination. Make a list of some of the wild ideas that you can imagine.

_____
_____
_____
_____
_____

Use your imagination to write a science fiction or fantasy poem. Start by jotting down several creative titles, such as "I Was Born on a Star" or "The Thing That Lives in My Closet" on the lines below.

_____
_____
_____

Now choose one of the titles and write a poem about it on the back of this page.

Exaggeration

Some poems use exaggeration or overstatement to make a point. When words are used to say one thing while the poem seems to say just the opposite, it is called **irony**.

I love homework and I always will.
What could be more fun than slaving over my desk all night
Away from the television.
Homework saves me from having to
Play baseball and other awful sports I'm good at.
If I had my choice I would rather do homework than eat
chocolate.

Try writing a poem called "Recycling" in which you use exaggeration to tell the world how *NOT* to recycle. Include as much irony as you can, and have fun!

_____

_____

_____

_____

_____

Irony is also the result of a combination of circumstances which turn out the opposite of the way they were intended. Take, for instance, the case of a college student who is so afraid of doing badly on a test that she stays up all night studying. The student goes to sleep feeling confident of knowing all the answers and then, because she is so tired, she sleeps through the alarm bell and misses the test entirely. That is irony. All that studying resulted in disaster.

Exaggeration is also used in satire. **Satire** is a little different from irony in that there is usually a target at which the writer is aiming. The writer will use ridicule, sarcasm, and irony to expose or attack something he or she does not like. An example of political satire is the editorial cartoons in the newspaper. Some aspect of politics is exaggerated to gain the desired effect.

Think of a national habit you do not like. What are some specific things you don't like about it? _____
Exaggerate those things and use them in a satirical poem on the lines below.

Example: The light turns yellow which must mean to speed
            because the man in that car is bearing down on me.

_____

_____

_____

_____

         POETRY WRITING

Multicultural Poetry

Skills:

a. understanding the richness of cultural diversity
b. writing Native American-type poetry
c. tapping students' backgrounds for poetry

Vocabulary:

multicultural, ancestry

Preparation:

Discuss the meaning of the word *multicultural*. If possible, make a chart of all the countries from which students' ancestors came.

Ask for information about Native Americans including why they are no longer called Indians, how they once lived, how they live now, etc.

Read and discuss poems written by Native Americans.

Extension Activities:

En Chanting!

Have students provide a background (with drums, etc.) for Native American poetry. Have students research Native American chants and mythology and then write poetry that shares some of the characteristics of these works. Students' books of Native American verse can be illustrated with masks, shields and other appropriate designs. A study of the different types of art from various tribes can be combined with a study of Native American poetry.

Poetry From Many Lands

After learning about their own heritage, students can find poetry by or about the people and customs which are part of their background. They can also write poetry about their backgrounds which can be included in an illustrated anthology.

Video Poetry

Show videos of other cultures. Have students write poems about the people and their environment.

Recitations

Old spirituals can be played or hummed as Langston Hughes' poetry is recited. Poems such as "The Dream Keeper" or "Mother to Son" would work well.

New Blues

Bring in and share a recording of a blues song. Then have students write their own blues lyrics.

Here is an example:

Wake up in the mornin'
I jump out of bed.
Ain't got my homework
Played football instead.
I've got the wakin' up early,
going to school tired, blues.

Bulletin Board:

Have students create individual coats of arms depicting their cultural backgrounds and other interests. Display them.

Books to Look for:

Niatum, Duane. ed., *Carriers of the Dream Wheel: Contemporary Native American Poetry.* Harper and Row, 1975.

Bierheist, John, ed,. *In the Trails of the Winds: American Indian Poems and Ritual Orations.* Straus and Giroux, 1971.

Baron, Virginia Olson. ed., *Here I Am!: An Anthology of Poems Written by Young People in Some of America's Minority Groups.* E.P. Dutton, 1969.

Cornish and Dixon. eds., *Chicory: Young Voices from the Black Ghetto.* Association Press.

Brooks, Gwendolyn. *Bronzeville Boys and Girls.* Harper, 1956.

Multicultural Poetry

Long before there was an alphabet, there was poetry. People expressed themselves in chants, songs and stories in order to make sense of their world and tell of their delights, hopes and fears. Poets came from every land and spoke every language.

Native Americans have left a rich legacy of art and traditions. There are Native Americans writing poetry today that reflects the pride and the sadness of people who are trying to survive in the modern world while keeping alive the old traditions and values.

Using words from the following list, write a poem which you believe a Native American might write today.

drums	people	walk	fire	sing
carving	mountain	trails	clouds	river
roots	home	moccasins	logs	heart
earthen	smoke	lodge	buckskin	old
ancient	feather	leather	water	chant
game	arrows	days	nights	moon
tepee	headband	beads	twine	sky
weaving	needle	bone	dawn	sun
dusk	corn	stars	nature	herbs

_____

_____

_____

_____

_____

_____

_____

_____

_____

_____

More Multicultural Poetry

Everyone has a unique background, ancestry, environment and history. Even twins have separate personalities, thoughts, experiences and desires. Each poet has his or her own "song to sing," but because we all share common feelings and emotions, we can relate to the writing of others.

Think of what is special about you and your family. What special things does your family always do at certain times of the year? On the lines below describe two or three of your family traditions.

_____

_____

_____

_____

What special foods have become traditional in your family? _____

_____

How does it make you feel when you and your family are following your traditions?

_____

In what ways are you like any of your relatives? _____

_____

In what ways are you different from them? _____

_____

What do you care deeply about? _____

_____

_____

Write a poem no one else but you could write.

_____

_____

_____

_____

_____

Haiku, Senryu and More

Skills:

Understanding and writing haiku, senryu, tanka, renga, and lanterne

Vocabulary:

haiku, senryu, tanka, renga, lanterne

Preparation:

If possible, take your class outside to make notes on nature and the signs of the present season. You may also choose to show slides or pictures of natural items such as birds, a sunrise, weather, etc.

Extension Activities:

Guess the Season

Have students write haiku about seasons without using the name of the season in the poem. Then have the rest of the class guess what season is depicted.

Senryu Later, Alligator!

Challenge students to write funny messages in the form of a senryu. Read some of the more amusing ones to the class.

Tanka Time

The *tanka* is a haiku with two extra lines of seven syllables each added at the end. Like haiku, tankas are about nature. Inform students that the last two lines are supposed to give a conclusive feeling to the poem.

Renga With a Group

The *renga* is a Japanese poem which is written by several people. The following activity will help students to learn its form. Divide students into groups. Begin by having one student write a haiku. Then have another student add two lines of 7 syllables each to the haiku. Another student should then add a haiku to the poem, and the next person adds two lines of 7 syllables. Continue adding to the poem until each group member has participated in the process. (A renga is a series of tankas.)

This works well with cooperative learning groups in which all group members help edit and proofread the poem before it is pronounced finished.

Light a Lanterne

The lanterne is a five-line poem with a 1, 2, 3, 4, 1 syllable pattern. It winds up looking like a Japanese lantern.

> *The*
> *old book*
> *is tattered*
> *but I love it*
> *best.*

Bulletin Board:

- Have students print lanternes on lantern-shaped paper. Then hang the lanternes and invite a neighboring class to come in and read them.
- Have students start off each month of the school year with a haiku reflecting what is happening in nature at that time of the year. Choose one (or more) and display it on the bulletin board surrounded by student illustrations.

Books to Look for:

Mizumira, Katzue. *Flower Moon Snow: A Book of Haiku.* Crowell, 1977.
Atwood, Ann. *Haiku: The Mood of Earth.* Charles & Sons, 1971.

Activity Sheet Answers (p. 29):

1. Spring
2. The daffodil grows in spring.

Haiku and Senryu

Haiku was originally the beginning part of a set of linked verses called *haikai*. These verses have been written in Japan since the sixteenth century. The haiku, which is very popular in Japan, has been increasing in popularity in the United States.

The haiku is valued for its simplicity. It is a three-line poem about nature. The first and third lines contain five syllables. The second line contains seven syllables.

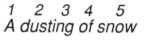

1 2   3   4   5
A dusting of snow

Covers the daffodil now

Smothering my heart.

Read the haiku above and number the syllables in lines two and three the way those in line one have been numbered. Answer the following questions.

1. What season does the above haiku refer to? _____

2. Why do you think it is that season? _____

Here is a haiku written by a student named Annie Wersching when she was in the fourth grade.

Snowflakes in winter
Fall down softly on the ground
All in different shapes.

Write a haiku to describe each of the four seasons.

_____   _____

_____   _____

_____   _____

_____   _____

_____   _____

_____   _____

A **senryu** is a poem which follows the haiku form, but does not have to be about nature.

Baseball is tempting   *Taking out the trash*
As I stare out the window   *Is as boring as it gets*
Across my math book.   *Except for sleeping.*

On the back of this page, write two senryu about topics that interest you.

Modern Poetry

Skills:

a. understanding modern poetry
b. writing modern poetry

Vocabulary:

prose, line breaks

Preparation:

Give each student a copy of a paragraph from an original story. Instruct them to try to make the story into a poem by breaking the prose into lines. The results, bland and disjointed phrases, will help show that modern poetry is not just prose broken into short lines.

Extension Activities:

"I Remember" Poems

This is a great starter activity for writing free verse. Have students write ten lines of poetry. Each line begins with "I remember." Next, instruct them to choose five or six favorite lines, cut out unnecessary words, and add other images and descriptions. Share the results.

There You Are/Here I Am

Have students write a fictitious poem to someone who has gone away. Tell students to describe the absent person and then tell what life is like since the person has gone. Urge kids to be creative with the names of places and other details.

There you are in New Orleans
writing postcards, seeing the shows,
and shopping at the French market.
You're eating crawfish and slurping gumbo
while I'm here at home, taking out the trash.

"I" Poems

Have students list things they like: activities they like to do, clubs they belong to, events they

have experienced, etc. Then have them write a poem containing their information.

I love lizards, and cats with long, soft fur.
I am nuts about hot fudge and french fries,
but not usually in the same dish.
I sing with the radio all the time,
but I'm shaky when I sing in public.
I am happiest on a horse or by a roaring fire.
I long to roam the woods, but I like to shop,
  too.
I listen to crazy country music and fast
  classical.
I never get enough of fiction and poetry.
I wear denim and turquoise,
and I wish I were part Cherokee.

Riddle Poems

Have students think of an object and then write clues in poetic lines as Anne Carkeet did with this poem she wrote in fifth grade. Notice how descriptive the language is without the use of words such as *ice cream* or *fudge sauce*.

What Am I?
I'm a dark brown river
Flowing down a mound
Of white billowing softness
Small brown chunks of rock
Are in my way
Then I come to a white mountain
All of a sudden I hit a rock
There is a ball of red
at the top
(Answer: a sundae)

Books to Look for:

Worth, Valerie. *Still More Small Poems*. Farrar, Strauss and Giroux, 1978.

Reflections on a Gift of Watermelon Pickle: And Other Modern Verse. Lothrop, Lee & Shepard Co., 1967.

Some Haystacks Don't Even Have Any Needle: And Other Complete Modern Poems. Scott, Foresman and Co., 1969.

Modern Poetry

Some people think modern poetry is simply prose divided up into lines so it looks like a poem. Actually, good modern poetry has a rhythm and often contains words that rhyme or echo through the lines. Line breaks are chosen carefully so that the words at the beginnings and ends of lines have great power or emphasis.

The punctuation in modern poetry is rather relaxed. Some poems contain no capital letters, others capitalize the first letter in each line. The punctuation style is determined by the poet, and should be consistent throughout the poem so it does not break a reader's concentration. Some punctuation, such as periods and commas, are included in order to cause a reader to pause at appropriate times. Readers also pause slightly at the end of each line.

Writing is often more effective when a writer cares deeply about a subject, rather than when a writer is trying to create a "great work." This author writes about something she has wanted for a long, long time.

When I was a child, I cried and sighed for
Horses.
I loved their smell, their eyes,
the way they thundered across a meadow
and how their long manes flagged as they flew.

I dreamed horse dreams and wrote horse stories,
clipped horse pictures from magazines.
I went to horse movies and saved my money
for plastic models of
Horses.

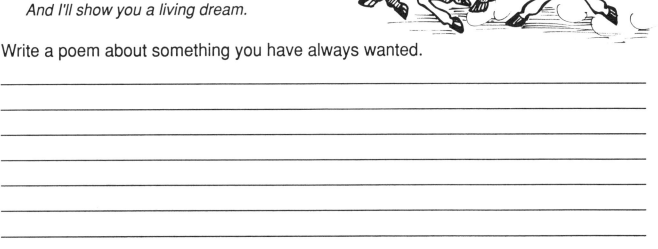

Now that I'm older you might think
I've outgrown
Horses.
Well, step on out to the barn with me
And I'll show you a living dream.

Write a poem about something you have always wanted.

_____

_____

_____

_____

_____

_____

_____

_____

     POETRY WRITING

Lyric Poems and Ballads

Skills:

a. understanding lyric poems and ballads
b. writing lyric poems and ballads

Vocabulary:

lyric, ballad, nostalgic

Preparation:

Bring in used greeting cards which contain good examples of lyric poetry. Read several aloud and ask how this poetry differs from other poetry students have studied. (expresses feelings, is personal, often about love and caring, uses personal pronouns, song-like quality to it, etc.)

You may choose to read or reproduce the following ballad for students:

Barbara Allen
'Twas in the merry month of May
When green buds all were swellin',
Sweet William on his death bed lay
For the love of Barbara Allen.

He sent his servant to the town,
To the place where she was dwellin'
Saying, "You must come to my master dear,
If your name be Barb'ry Allen."

So, slowly, slowly she got up,
And slowly she drew nigh him,
And the only words to him did say,
"Young man, I think you're dyin'."

He turned his face unto the wall,
And death was in him wellin',
"Good-bye, good-bye to my friends all,
Be good to Barb'ry Allen."

When he was dead and laid in grave,
She heard the death bells knellin',
And every stroke to her did say:
"Hard-hearted Barb'ry Allen."

"Oh Mother, oh Mother, go dig my grave,
Make it both long and narrow.
Sweet William died of love for me,
And I will die of sorrow."

"And Father, oh Father, go dig my grave,
Make it both long and narrow.
Sweet William died on yesterday,
And I will die tomorrow."

Barb'ry Allen was buried in the old churchyard.
Sweet William was buried beside her.
Out of Sweet William's heart there grew a rose,
Out of Barb'ry Allen's, a briar.

They grew and grew in the old churchyard,
'Til they could grow no higher.
At the end they formed a true lovers' knot,
And the rose grew 'round the briar.

Discuss the ballad's beginning, middle and end and its rhyme scheme. Ask students if they can find a metaphor in the last stanza.

Extension Activities:

Ballad Charades!
After a study of many ballads, play charades with the titles.

From Movie to Song
Have students work in pairs or small groups to take favorite movies and turn them into ballads.

Ballad as Story
Use ballads as a way to show the importance of beginning, middle, and end. Have kids write a synopsis or outline of an entire ballad.

Books to Look for:

Blishen, Edward. *Oxford Book of Poetry for Children*. Bedrick Books, 1984.
Benet, Stephen Vincent. *Ballads and Poems*. Holt, Rinehart and Winston, 1959.

Activity Sheet Answers (p. 33):

1. Singer is sentimental about times past.
2. last line
3. Rhythm, rhyme and repetition

Lyric Poems and Ballads

The winds may blow upon the salted seas
and whip the waves into a frenzied froth
But we will sail in heavy boats that breeze
through roughened water like a sword through cloth.

   The lyric poem expresses feelings and has a song-like quality to it. Lyric poetry is often about life and love, and quite commonly contains images from nature. Lyric poetry is used in greeting cards and songs, as well as in letters and verses to loved ones. Lyric poetry often uses personal pronouns (I, you, we, us, etc.).

   Write a four-line lyric poem for a greeting card for the occasion of your choice. Use the characteristics of the lyric poem described in the paragraph above.

_____

_____

_____

_____

   The **ballad** is a simple lyric poem which tells a story. The story is often romantic or nostalgic, and the ballad is often set to music, like "Old Blue." This ballad is of unknown origin, but is widely known throughout the rural southern area of the United States.

Had a dog and his name was Blue
Had a dog and his name was Blue
Had a dog and his name was Blue
Betcha five dollars he's a good un' too.

Come on Blue, you good dog you.

Shouldered my gun and I tooted my horn,
Gonna find a possum in the new-ground corn,
Old Blue barked and I went to see,
Cornered a 'possum up in a tree.

Come on Blue, you good dog you.

Old Blue died, and he died so hard,
Shook the ground in my back yard,
Dug his grave with a silver spade,
Lowered him down with links of chain.

Every link, I did call his name,
Here, Blue, you good dog, you,
Here, Blue, I'm comin' there too.

1. Why could this poem be described as nostalgic? _____

_____

2. Which line suggests that the man believes he and his dog will be together again someday? _____

3. What aspects of this ballad would make a reader suspect that it is often sung?

_____

_____

4. Write a ballad patterned after "Old Blue." Use the rhyme scheme AABB. Your ballad should tell a story about something sentimental.

Rhyme Time

Skills:

a. understanding and writing rhyme
b. understanding external and internal rhyme

Vocabulary:

external rhyme, internal rhyme

Preparation:

Many students enjoy rhyming words. One simple exercise is to put a word on the board and go around the room requesting a rhyming word from one student after another. List the words on the chalkboard. Then write a new word on the board and have the children make their own lists of rhyming words.

Ask what poetic advertising jingles students can think of. Discuss why rhymed ads can be effective.

Extension Activities:

Rhyme Cards
On index cards write words that are easily rhymed. Shuffle the cards and pass them out, one to each student. Have students write 12 to 20 words that rhyme with their starter words. Collect the starter words, then hand them out again. Have students create a rhyming poem which includes many of the words on the card they receive. (Good rhyming words include *goat, quail, fox, tune, splat, nest* and *fill*.)

Rhyme Rounds
Have students sit in a circle. Call out a word that rhymes with many other words. The entire group should slap hands on thighs, clap hands once, then a student says a word that rhymes with the word. Students slap thighs and clap hands, then the next student says a rhyming word. Continue in this way around the circle until someone misses. The last person who correctly rhymes the word becomes the leader.

Playing with Rhyme
Have students work in small groups to rewrite popular nursery rhymes in silly or creative ways. Emphasize that the final products should still rhyme.

Wallpaper Rhymes
Have students print rhyming words on construction paper with markers. Tape the paper on the classroom walls to create a pattern.

Timed Rhymes
Put children in groups and have contests to see which group can list the most rhyming words in a given time. Then the groups can write poems which contain the words.

Borrowed Rhyme
Have students make lists of rhyming words from published poems and then use them to create their own poetry.

Bulletin Board:

Out of white paper cut several dog shapes large enough to hold many large spots. In each spot, place a word that rhymes with that dog's name. For example, a dog named Spot might have *pot, cot, tot, trot, lot, jot, plot*, etc.

Books to Look for:

Redfield, Bessie. *Capricorn Rhyming Dictionary*. Perigree, 1986.
Webster's Compact Rhyming Dictionary. Merriam-Webster, 1987.
Kuskin, Karla. *Dogs and Dragons, Trees and Dreams*. Harper and Row, 1980.

Activity Sheet Answers (p. 36):

I'd like to take a ride in a hot air balloon
and float up wide-eyed into the sky.
High above the world in an air-filled ball
my lips are curled in a satisfied smile!

Name _____

Rhyme Time

Poetry does not have to rhyme, but many poems do. The first poems that many children learn are nursery rhymes. Children delight in hearing the pattern and meter of these old poems.

Pattycake, pattycake, baker's man
Bake me a cake as fast as you can.
Prick it and pat it and mark it with a B.
Put it in the oven for Baby and me.

The first poems we write are often based on simple rhymes:

I love cats   *I love dogs*
I love bats   *I love hogs*
I love hats and   *I love frogs and*
I love rats.   *Lincoln logs!*

It is not only the rhyme, but the beat of the rhythm that is enjoyable. If you tap out the rhythm of the poem above, how many taps per line do you get? 3-3-4-3 That is also the number of syllables in the poem. Now write your own poem using the same meter, or number of beats per line.

_____   _____

_____   _____

_____   _____

_____   _____

The pattern of rhyme in a poem is called its rhyme scheme. We mark the pattern with letters of the alphabet.

Freezing rain had sealed the window panes	A	*Cats love fish.*	A
While I was stranded with ten candy canes.	A	*Dogs love bones.*	B
Father is a chef and wants to bake.	B	*Pigs love mud.*	C
But here I am with this dumb stomach ache.	B	*And kids love cones.*	B

Choose one of the rhyme schemes above, or try a rhyme scheme of ABBA and write your poem on the lines below.

_____

_____

_____

_____

Rhyme Time, Too

I'm supposed to sweep the floor and carefully clean my room.
But luckily for me my dog just ate the only broom.
I'm expected to have supper waiting on the table
But since I have this sick old dog, I do not think I'm able.

When the rhyme occurs at the ends of lines as it does in the poem above it is called **external rhyme**. On the lines below, list four sets of rhyming words which would be fun to use in a poem.

_____ _____ _____ _____

_____ _____ _____ _____

_____ _____ _____ _____

_____ _____ _____ _____

Now write a poem using words from your list above to create an external rhyming pattern.

_____

_____

_____

_____

_____

When rhyme occurs within the lines of a poem, it is called **internal rhyme**. Here is a poem with internal rhyme:

I'd like to take a ride in a hot air balloon
and float up wide-eyed into the sky.
High above the world in an air-filled ball
my lips are curled in a satisfied smile!

Underline the words that make up the poem's internal rhyme.

Now it is your turn to write a poem with internal rhyme. You may not only use exact rhymes, but also words that echo the same vowel sounds such as *sky* and *smile*.

_____

_____

_____

_____

_____

Couplets, Sonnets & More

Skills:
a. understanding the English sonnet
b. understanding and writing couplets, tercets, triplets, and quatrains

Vocabulary:

sonnet, iambic pentameter, couplets, tercet, triplet, quatrain

Preparation:

Discuss the fact that iambic pentameter is much like natural speech. Have students read the worksheet sonnet silently, then read it aloud to them. Finally, have students break into groups and plan choral readings with group members taking parts.

Extension Activities:

Crazy Couplets
Couplets consist of two rhyming lines, usually of equal length, that are fairly easy to write. Ask students to write humorous couplets of varying length.

> *I met a gypsy in a shoe*
> *who said her name was Blister Blue.*

Closed Couplets
Closed couplets are couplets that are complete poems. Have students write three closed couplets and decide as a class which are truly complete.

> *Never swim without a friend.*
> *You might meet a lonely end.*

Multi-couplets
Poems may contain an unlimited number of couplets.

> *I saw a cat who had three eyes*
> *Which was a very great surprise.*

> *The cat was laughing at a dog*
> *Which had a snout just like a hog.*

> *The dog was looking right at me*
> *So I just stepped behind a tree.*

Ask students to write poems containing at least four couplets.

Try a Tercet
A tercet is three lines that may be put together in varying rhyme patterns (AAB; AB A, etc.). When all three lines end in the same rhyme, they are called triplets.

> *Jimmy Joe the lumberjack*
> *Carried logs in his knapsack*
> *until he had a mile-high stack!*

Ask students to write a triplet on the subject of something they like or dislike.

Quatrain Training
The quatrain is a popular rhyming form of poetry. It is made up of four lines and the rhyme pattern can vary. The rhyme scheme is marked with letters of the alphabet. *A* stands for the first end rhyme, *B* for the second, etc.

> *Helen Haley climbed a tree (A)*
> *With a hammer, nails, and me. (A)*
> *We built a tree house way up high (B)*
> *And then came down chased by a bee! (A)*

> *My unicorn has golden wings (A)*
> *And softest mane and tail. (B)*
> *He flies through clouds and always brings (A)*
> *Me letters by air mail! (B)*

Ask students to write quatrains with varying rhyme patterns.

Books to Look for:

Blishen, Edward. *Oxford Book of Poetry for Children*. Bedrick Books, 1984.

Activity Sheet Answers (p. 38):

1 and 5 contain the meter used in English sonnets

Simple Sonnets and Couplets

Three cats are sitting on my window sill,
One black, one grey, one tortoise-shell with white.
They don't belong to me. I've had my fill
Of felines shrieking wildly in the night.

Two dogs are growling underneath the cats.
They jump and snap with teeth like sharpened wires.
These dogs belong to someone who likes spats
And doesn't mind the way the dogs chase tires.

One guinea pig is nibbling at the sage
with beaver jaw and nose of wiggling brown.
Its owner will not put it in a cage
So gardens suffer all across the town.

It's time to leave this pet-infested place,
As soon as they stop licking at my face!

This is an **English sonnet**. It contains fourteen lines and has definite meter and rhyme. It is often called the Shakespearean sonnet because William Shakespeare was the greatest writer of this form. The English sonnet has the rhyme scheme a-b-a-b, c-d-c-d, e-f-e-f, g-g. The English sonnet is written in **iambic pentameter**. This means there are five iambs (unstressed syllable followed by stressed syllable) in each line. In simple language, every line sounds like ta dah, ta dah, ta dah, ta dah, ta dah. "I **al**ways **wear** a **hel**met **when** I **ride**." The first line of the sonnet above would be marked:

Three cats are sitting on my window sill.

Other famous writers who wrote in this poetic form are John Milton, Elizabeth Barrett Browning, and American poet Edna St. Vincent Millay.

Put an *x* in the blank before the lines which contain the meter used in English sonnets.

1. _____ How glad she was to see him in the fall.
2. _____ Seven silly sidecars sat in the cycle shop.
3. _____ She skates on a layer of sparkling ice.
4. _____ With a hey and a ho and hey, hey, ho.
5. _____ The forest is a wild and blooming place.

The sonnet on this page ends in a couplet, the oldest rhyming form. A **couplet** is simply two lines, usually equal in length, that rhyme.

If you put your saddle backwards on your horse
You will see ahead what is behind, of course.

On the back of this paper, write a couplet in iambic pentameter.

38

Fine-Tuning Your Poems

Skills:
guiding a poem through the revision process

Preparation:

If possible, have a poet come in to talk to the class about rewriting and to show students the vast number of drafts from which a single poem may evolve.

The corresponding worksheet (p. 40) can be used by students throughout the school year as they revise the poems they write.

Extension Activities:

Editing Table
Designate a table or spare desk in the classroom for the editing of written work. Stock it with scissors, tape, paper for final drafts, highlighters, red pens, and copies of the Fine Tuning activity sheet.

Poetry Puzzle
Write the following poem in paragraph form and copy it for students. Have them work in pairs to reconstruct the poem. Explain that there is no right way to do it, just a way that sounds the best to them and conveys the meaning intended by the poet. Have students defend their reasons for the line breaks they chose.

Point out the pun in the title. The word *heart* is a play on the word *art* as in a work of art. Discuss how the title adds meaning to the poem.

A Work of Heart
A poem is a reaching out
and trying to understand
why you are you
and I am me,
like holding out your hand.

A poem is a work of art
with colors, shapes and lines.
It may not be
a Rembrandt oil
but it will be all mine.

Group Rewrite
Write a poem that highlights certain skills your class needs. Put it on the overhead or chalkboard. Revise the poem with the class, calling on various students for changes they would make and reasons changes are needed.

Revision Teams
After working extensively on revising their own poetry, send your students to lower grades to help younger students write and revise poems.

Editing Skills Groups
Divide students into editing skills groups based on their strengths. For example, if a student needs spelling help, he/she can visit the spelling skills group. For help with commas, a student can visit the punctuation group. Different skills can include line breaks, rhyme, alliteration, grammar, meter, and others dictated by your group's needs.

Student Teachers
One of the best ways to learn something is to teach it. Have students work in groups of five or six to put together presentations for other classes on how to revise poetry. Have groups "practice" on one another until they are ready to "take the show on the road."

Bulletin Board:

Display first and final drafts of poems. If available, tack up a series of drafts of the same poem.

Fine-Tuning Your Poems

When you think a poem is finished, it is time to give it a close look. Do a bit of tightening here. Add a touch of color there. Make the poem sound and look as good as you can. This page will take you from first draft to finished product.

Think of something that happened to you when you were younger. Write a poem about it without judging anything you are writing. Later, you can remove any parts you don't like. If you follow where your thoughts lead, you will have fun with the poem and write some interesting things.

Robert Frost said, "A poem begins in delight and ends in wisdom." What does that mean? Try to make your poems delightful and satisfying.

After you have written your poem, answer the following questions, making the necessary changes to the poem as you go.

1. Read your poem silently. Is the entire poem about one subject? If not, remove extra parts to use later in another poem.
2. Now read the poem aloud, pausing slightly at the end of each line. Are the line breaks in the right places so that your reader will read the poem as you intend it to be read?
3. Are there any clichés (old tired words or phrases) you could change to something more original?
4. Which lines "sing" and which lines lie flat? What can you change so that every line does a job and is interesting in some way?
5. Does the title add something to the poem or echo the mood? It should.
6. Is the poem complete? Do you need to say more?
7. Are there clear images in your poem?
8. Are your verbs strong? Try not to use forms of the verb *to be* (*was*, *were*, etc.). Choose more interesting and descriptive verbs.
9. Have you used too many adjectives or adverbs? (Which is more interesting "The soot-black cat walked slowly and stiffly up behind the brown, speckled bird." or "The ebony cat stalked the sparrow" ?
10. Are you satisfied with your poem and its meaning? Even if you dislike a poem you have written, do not throw it away. Instead, underline the parts you like and use them in another poem.

       POETRY WRITING

Celebrate Poetry!

Skills:
a. writing poetry for a class anthology
b. designing and proofreading a cover

Preparation:

Classroom anthologies make wonderful records of student writing to keep in the classroom, send home to parents, or keep in the school library. They are just one way of celebrating the poetry of your class.

Begin by sharing anthologies of poetry by other students or by professional poets.

Extension Activities:

Meet the Poet
Every six weeks introduce the class to a new poet. Share background information, poems, videos, photos, etc.

The Poets' Feast!
Arrange a special meal or party. The ticket to the feast is an original poem. You can have a theme around which the foods and poetry center.

Poetry Fair
Have each child research a poet and set up a display of information about the poet with samples of her or his work, tapes of the student reading the poetry, scenes from the poet's life, etc. Have other students and administrators attend.

Pick a Poet
Have each child draw the name of a poet from a hat. The student will then do research and present a short report on the poet.

Poetry Perils!
Tell the students they are being held in a creepy old castle by an ogre who responds only to poetry. Have them write a poem they could use to be released.

Poetry Column
Add a poetry column to your classroom or school newspaper.

Poetry Club
Start a poetry club. Meetings can be held during lunch or after school one night a week. A parent with an interest in poetry may be willing to attend or conduct meetings.

Announcing Poetry
If you have an intercom system, a daily or weekly poem reading is fun and inspirational.

Poetry Hour
Put on a poetry hour for other classes and /or parents. Use a theme and read either published poems or a combination of published poems and student poems. The latter is a wonderful method of giving student writers status as they perform their work together with that of published authors. Allowing children to choose and/or write the poetry presented (with the teacher's approval) helps involve them in the entire process.

This presentation can grow into a multimedia production including dancing, singing, music, artwork, slides (slides of student artwork can be a great background), etc.

Acting Out
Give several groups of students the same poem to perform. Then have students take turns performing it and enjoy the varied results.

A tape recorder can be used to supply sound effects. If possible, videotape the results and critique them with the actors. Puppet shows can be performed to dramatize a poem.

Bulletin Board:

Create a poetry bulletin board on which you display your students' poetry along with the verse of published poets, parents, teachers (including yourself), administrators, etc.

Celebrate Poetry!

Poetry is an expression of the human spirit reaching out to communicate with others. It deserves to be celebrated. One way to celebrate poetry is with a party. Another way is by publishing poetry.

Here is an excerpt from a poem in an anthology, or collection, of children's poems. The children wrote about their experiences at sixth-grade camp. The student author's name is Jon Wiswall.

My camping memories, oh how fond!
The coldness of Mud Cave's mud pond
Plays back and back again
To make me wonder which branch
Of the Mississippi we were in.

Piranha-eye mamas, what a happy thought,
Gave me the thrills and challenge I sought.
And because of that, I hope I never need to go
Into the Amazon unless it's a Disney ride, you know.

Write a poem for your class anthology. Write the poem about something special you did with your class this year. Be specific and descriptive. Try to bring alive the memory so that if a classmate read your poem five years from now, he or she would clearly remember this year.

_____

_____

_____

_____

_____

_____

Now design a cover for the anthology.

Don't forget to include the following:
- grade level
- name of school
- date
- activity
- city and state
- illustrations

When you are finished with the design, ask a classmate to help you proofread for spelling mistakes.

A Poem a Day for 40 Days

The following list contains miscellaneous poetry ideas that can be used throughout the school year. Feel free to adapt them to the specific needs of your group. Additional poetry ideas for each month of the year can be found on pages 45 – 47. Enjoy!

1. After a study of mythology, have students write poems about the myths or about a mythological character.
2. Write historical poems. Historical poems describe an historical event. *Paul Revere's Ride* by Henry Wadsworth Longfellow is an example of an historical poem.
3. Write a poem that could be used as a commercial.
4. Write rhyming poems (or songs) which explain grammar or spelling rules.
5. Write poems about playing a musical instrument.
6. Write poems about vacations.
7. Write poems about favorite colors, animals, etc.
8. Write poems about food.
9. Write poems about excuses.
10. Write poems about saving the rainforest.
11. Write poems about famous paintings.
12. Write a poem in which you speak about yourself in the third person (he, she).
13. Write poetry while listening to sound effects of whales or other sounds of nature.
14. Write a poem about something you don't do well.
15. Write a poem about what "bugs" you the most.
16. Write an impossibly difficult poem.
17. Write a perfectly simple poem.
18. Write a poem with absolutely no adjectives or adverbs.
19. Write a poem with absolutely no verbs.
20. Write a poem with absolutely no nouns.
21. Write a poem about a ghost.
22. Write a poem about your least favorite food.
23. Write a poem based on a newspaper headline.
24. Write a poem requesting a raise in your allowance.
25. Write a poem describing a very silly sight.
26. Take a rhymed poem you have written and rewrite it in free verse.
27. Rewrite one of your poems that doesn't rhyme so that it rhymes.
28. Write a poem just for yourself. You do not have to share it with anyone. Write the poem in whatever form you wish. Underline your favorite parts of the poem.
29. Pretend you are something from nature, such as a mountain, tree or river. Write a poem from that item's point of view. (example: "The sun greens my leaves...")
30. Write a familiar fairy tale in the form of a poem.
31. Write a funny poem. If it makes you laugh, it will usually make others laugh. Try it out on your friends.
32. Write a poem for a phone answering machine! It's very practical!
33. Write a narrative poem—a poem that tells a story.
34. Write a poem about your most embarrassing moment.
35. Write a poem about your ideal day.
36. Write a song about school.
37. Write a poem of celebration.
38. Write a poem in which you use a train trip as a metaphor for your life.
39. Write a poem about beginnings and endings.
40. Write a poem that tells what you have learned about poems. Try to teach your readers something about poetry.

Group Poems

Most poems are written by individuals who work independently to create a piece of writing. During this activity, however, you will work with other students to create group poems.

Form a small group of five or six students. Every student in the group will write the first line or two of a poem. Next, he or she will pass the paper to the person on his or her left. The new writer will read what the first writer has written and add another line or two to the poem. Then the papers will be passed on to the next writer in the group, and so on. Note that all writers must stay with the subject and style chosen by the first writer. For example, if the first few lines of the poem rhyme, additional lines must also rhyme. The last person to receive a poem must write lines that conclude the poem, then return the poem to the writer of the first lines. That poet will edit the entire poem and prepare a final copy of it.

Write your name on the top line below then begin your poem.

A poem started by _____

_____

_____

_____

_____

_____

_____

_____

_____

_____

_____

_____

_____

_____

_____

Seasonal Poetry Ideas (January – April)

JANUARY

1. Write a poem beginning "Here I am in January..."
2. Write a poem about New Year's resolutions. Include silly or fun resolutions in your poem.
3. January is National Hobby Month. Write a poem about your favorite hobby.
4. Elvis Presley was born January 8, 1935. He was often referred to as "the king." Write a poem about a nickname you would or wouldn't want to have.
5. January 15 is Martin Luther King's birthday. Write a poem about freedom or equality.

FEBRUARY

1. Write a narrative poem (one that tells a story) about a groundhog that wouldn't leave its hole. Be sure the poem has a beginning, middle and end. How might this groundhog's behavior affect the people who believe that if the groundhog sees its shadow there will be six more weeks of winter?
2. February 12 is Abraham Lincoln's birthday. He was born in 1809. In honor of this famous president, write a letter poem to today's president giving him some advice on how to be a good president.
3. Write a Valentine's Day poem to yourself.
4. February 22 is George Washington's birthday. It is said that he never lied, even when he was in trouble. Let's make an exception to his rule about lying. Write a silly poem filled with lies and exaggerations.

MARCH

1. Think about the types of clothing you wear in different weather. Write a poem that contains rules about what to wear during different seasons.
2. In honor of St. Patrick's Day, write a limerick about your favorite or least favorite school subject.
3. March is often a windy month. Make a list of five harmful things the wind can do and five good things the wind can do. Then write a poem about March wind.
4. Write a silly poem about how March received its name.
5. Haiku are three-line poems. The first line contains five syllables, the second line contains seven, and the third line contains five. Haiku are usually about nature. Write a haiku about today's weather.

APRIL

1. April first is the traditional day to play practical jokes on friends and relatives. Invent a new and harmless practical joke. Write a poem about the joke and what might happen if you played it on someone.
2. Washington Irving was born in April of 1783. He wrote "The Legend of Sleepy Hollow," about Ichabod Crane who was chased by the "headless horseman." Write a silly poem about the advantages and disadvantages of being headless.
3. Write several Haiku poems about April rain.
4. April is Keep America Beautiful Month. Write a poem recommending ways to keep America from being buried under a stack of litter.
5. The first public school kindergarten was founded in 1873 in St. Louis, Missouri. Do you remember what kindergarten was like? Try writing a poem about the joys and sorrows of being in kindergarten.

Seasonal Poetry Ideas (May – August)

MAY

1. May is National Sleep Month. Many people must have certain conditions in place before they can sleep. Some people want closet doors closed. Others like to wear a favorite garment. Some people need two pillows; some use none. What are your rules for a good night's sleep? Write them in the form of a poem.
2. A gift most mothers like better than any other is something created by their children. Think about the things you like best about your mother, your stepmother, your grandmother, or a person who often takes care of you. Write a poem to or about this person. Consider giving it as a gift.
3. Often around this time of year, children begin to think about the approaching summer vacation. Even the word *vacation* has an exciting ring to it. Make a list in which you describe vacation in twenty different ways. (Vacation is flying. Vacation is freedom.) Put your sentences in the order in which you think they sound best.
4. May is a good month for baseball. List all the words you can think of that have anything to do with baseball. Don't forget the action and sound words like *slide* and *smack*. Now write an action baseball poem.

JUNE

1. June is Dairy Month. Write a mouth-watering poem about your favorite dairy products!
2. Write an acrostic poem for your father, or for another man whom you admire, for Father's Day. Write the person's name down the left side of a piece of paper and write a word or phrase that describes him for each letter of his name (ex. H-andsome, A-always there, N-ice, K-icks football well).
3. June is Zoo Month! Think of some unusual occupants of the zoo. Write a poem about them.

JULY

1. It has been said that it's so hot in July in some places that people can fry an egg on the sidewalk. Think of other ways to let a reader know how hot it is in July and include those ways in a poem.
2. Henry David Thoreau was born in July. He was a famous naturalist who studied animals and nature. Pretend you are in the woods early on a July morning. Describe what you see, hear, and smell.
3. July is National Anti-Boredom Month. Write a wild, crazy, "non-boring" poem.

AUGUST

1. In many states, August is the month for state fairs. Along with livestock and agricultural contests and displays, there are usually many carnival rides. Write a poem about the wildest ride you can imagine.
2. On August 28, 1963, Dr. Martin Luther King, Jr. gave his famous "I Have a Dream" speech. Dr. King's dream was that people of all colors could get along together as equals. Think of what you want for your family, your school, your country or the world. What is your dream? Write a poem about your dream.
3. August is the end of summer vacation in many parts of the United States. Write a nostalgic poem (one which recalls the season with fondness) in which you say farewell to summer and hello to autumn.
4. Make a list of all the places you have visited or fun activities you have done this summer. Choose one to write about in a poem.

Seasonal Poetry Ideas (September – December)

SEPTEMBER

1. The first Labor Day in the United States was celebrated on Tuesday, September 5, 1882. Make a list of all the occupations you can think of in five minutes. Then include the most interesting ones in a poem.
2. A famous writer named O. Henry was born on September 11, 1862. O. Henry, whose actual name was William Sydney Porter, was the master of the surprise ending. One of his famous stories is "The Gift of the Magi." Write a poem that surprises readers with a twist or surprise at the end.
3. September is National Breakfast Month. Make a list of the names of your favorite breakfast foods. See which ones rhyme or almost rhyme. Then write a breakfast poem with a rhyme pattern of ABAB ABAB.

OCTOBER

1. The inventor of the air-brake, George Westinghouse, was born in October of 1846. He started giving his factory workers a half day off on Saturdays. Before that most people worked a six-day week. Write a Saturday poem.
2. October 15 is National Grouch Day. Write your grouchiest poem!
3. The last complete week in October is Cleaner Air Week. Write a poem about what the results could be if people worldwide do not take care of the air.
4. October 31 is Halloween. What kinds of words might be used in a Halloween poem? List as many words as possible that could be used in place of the word *scary*.

NOVEMBER

1. November 1 is Author's Day. Write a poem about your favorite author and/or about the author's books. Or, if you want to, write a poem about the kinds of books you would like to write and have published.
2. Thanksgiving is almost here. Instead of writing a poem about what you are thankful for, write a poem about all the things you have that you could do without.
3. On November 21, 1783, two Frenchmen Jean Francois Pilatre and Marquis Francois Laurent d'Arlandes became the first men to fly in a hot air balloon. Imagine that you were one of those men. It is your first time in the air, floating above farms and over trees. Write a poem about that first flight.
4. The first Tuesday in November is Election Day. Write a poem encouraging people to get out and vote.

DECEMBER

1. Write a poem about something made out of snow. Make the poem different from any snow song or poem you have ever heard.
2. Imagine yourself in a blizzard. Use all your senses. Now write a poem called "Blizzard."
3. December is a month in which many households keep holiday traditions that were started years ago. What are your traditions? Write a poem about your family traditions.

Name _____

Any-Season Poetry

1. Write an upbeat poem which tells about your hopes for this year.

   _____

   _____

   _____

   _____

   _____

   _____

   _____

   _____

2. We can make resolutions during any time of year. Write an acrostic poem with a resolution for each of the letters in the word *goal*. It can be a resolution for you, for a friend, or even for your pet! Here is an example:

   Get more sleep
   Offer to take out the trash
   Accept help with math without getting mad
   Let little sister play with video games

   G_____
   O_____
   A_____
   L_____

3. Sometimes in spring when people don't feel like working, they say spring fever is affecting them. Actually, the urge to take a break can hit any time of year. Think of three things you would rather do than work, then write a "spring fever" poem.

   _____

   _____

   _____

   _____

   _____

   _____

4. Maurice Sendak was born June 10, 1928. His book *Where the Wild Things Are* has delighted children for years. Think of a story or poem that delighted you when you were younger. Now on the back of this paper write a poem you think a young child would like.